LORD GREY OF THE REFORM BILL

By the same Author

ENGLAND IN THE AGE OF WYCLIFFE. 8vo.

GARIBALDI'S DEFENCE OF THE ROMAN REPUBLIC (1848-9). With 7 Maps and 35 Illustrations. 8vo.

GARIBALDI AND THE THOUSAND (May, 1860). With 5 Maps and numerous Illustrations. 8vo.

GARIBALDI AND THE MAKING OF ITALY (May–November, 1860). With 4 Maps and numerous Illustrations. 8vo.

LONGMANS, GREEN, AND CO.
LONDON   NEW YORK   BOMBAY
CALCUTTA AND MADRAS

Walter L. Colls. Sc.

Charles, 2nd Earl Grey, K.G.
1764–1845.
From the picture by Sir Thomas Lawrence at Howick.
about 1827.

LORD GREY OF THE REFORM BILL

BEING THE

LIFE OF CHARLES, SECOND EARL GREY

BY

GEORGE MACAULAY TREVELYAN

LATE FELLOW OF TRINITY COLLEGE, CAMBRIDGE

AUTHOR OF
' GARIBALDI, ETC.,' ' LIFE OF JOHN BRIGHT '
' SCENES FROM ITALY'S WAR '

*WITH PORTRAITS AND OTHER
ILLUSTRATIONS*

LONGMANS, GREEN, AND CO.
39 PATERNOSTER ROW, LONDON
FOURTH AVENUE & 30TH STREET, NEW YORK
BOMBAY, CALCUTTA, AND MADRAS
1920

To the Memory of
ALBERT, FOURTH EARL GREY
AT WHOSE DESIRE
THIS WORK WAS UNDERTAKEN

PREFACE

When the late Earl Grey invited me, in 1913, to make use of the Howick Papers, in order to write the life of his grandfather, I asked him whether I might be allowed a freedom of historical comment more extensive than would be proper in the biography of a statesman recently dead. The permission was granted with characteristic readiness and generosity. My work was interrupted by an interval of more than four years of war, during which the late Lord Grey died, but his son, in the same spirit, desired me to complete the book.

The original biography of the Reform Bill Premier, begun by his children for the benefit of a generation that had known him, was suspended midway,[1] and the work had to be undertaken afresh. After the lapse of so many decades, the nature of the task had changed. A very different book is now wanted from that which would have been welcomed at a time when Russell, Palmerston, and other leading actors in the conflict of the great Reform Bill were still in public life, and when the clubs were full of men who remembered the Prince Regent and the Rotten Boroughs. Many debates, incidents, and intrigues that convulsed Brooks's, and were long held in memory there, have now lost the halo of traditional interest, without acquiring historical importance. The biographer, for example, is no longer called upon to narrate in detail the series of once famous negotiations by which Grey evaded office between 1809 and 1812. On the other hand, the trend and change of middle and working class opinion during the forty years of

[1] *Some Account of the Life and Opinions of Charles, Second Earl Grey*, by Lieut.-Gen. Hon. C. Grey, 1861, goes no further than the year 1817.

the movement for Parliamentary Reform over which Grey presided, are of deeper interest than ever in the historical perspective of our own day, and give unity and permanent value to Lord Grey's career, as viewed down the lengthening ages.

For this reason I have not only used the rich treasury of the Howick Papers themselves, and the documents relative to my subject in Holland House and Lambton Castle, most kindly put at my disposition by Lord Ilchester and Lord Durham, but I have studied—among the Additional MSS. in the British Museum and among the Home Office Papers—the currents on which the ship of Reform was launched by Grey in the period of the first French Revolution, and the all-powerful but dangerous flood-tide on which he brought the vessel into harbour in 1832.

The object of the present volume is to recall the life of a great historical character to the public of our day. In an age when the law of perpetual and rapid change is accepted as inevitable, and the difficulty is to obtain progress without violence, there may be profit in the story of a statesman who, after a period of long stagnation and all too rigid conservatism, initiated in our country a yet longer period of orderly democratic progress, and at the critical moment of the transition averted civil war and saved the State from entering on the vicious circle of revolution and reaction.

I am grateful to Sir Algernon West for access to letters of Lady Grey, and to Lord Spencer for Grey's letters to Althorp. I am much indebted to Mr. and Mrs. Hammond for help and suggestions; and to Lord Halifax for putting at my disposal, with indefatigable kindness, his traditional knowledge of the Grey family in that period, and of the circle in which they moved.

G. M. TREVELYAN.

December, 1919.

CONTENTS

BOOK I

THE FORMATION OF PARTIES

BOOK II

THE STAGNATION OF PARTIES

BOOK III

THE REFORM BILL

APPENDICES

ILLUSTRATIONS

LORD GREY
OF THE REFORM BILL

BOOK I
THE FORMATION OF PARTIES

CHAPTER I

BOYHOOD AND YOUTH——WHIG SOCIETY AND POLITICS
ON THE EVE OF THE FRENCH REVOLUTION

' At an age when most of those who distinguish themselves in life are still contending for prizes and Fellowships at college, he had won for himself a conspicuous place in Parliament. At twenty-three he had been thought worthy to be ranked with the veteran statesmen who appeared as the delegates of the British Commons at the bar of the British nobility.'—MACAULAY ON CHARLES GREY.

THE map of Britain shows England thrusting up a wedge far northward along its eastern coast, to touch the Tweed and claim the Till. This extremity of Northumberland consists of a long belt of low country lying between the highest part of the Cheviots and the Northern Sea, arable along the coast, but some miles inland swelling up into moors. Moorland and arable alike are dominated by great presences—to the west the rounded mass of Cheviot Hill, and to the east the ocean, seen from every piece of rising ground when

B

the day is clear, while the west wind is for ever tearing
across, as a messenger between hills and sea.   Since
the days of Cuthbert on Holy Island it has been a
fine coast for the breeding and rearing of men.   It
could not have been held for England without hard
fighting, on a larger scale than in other parts of
Northumberland, for it was a royal highroad of inva-
sion between Scotland and England.   Names such as
Flodden and Etal, Bamborough and Dunstanborough,
Alnwick and Warkworth recall, not the bickerings of
border outlaws, but the strife of two great Kingdoms.
In all this work the Greys had their full share.   But,
although they possessed land at Howick from 1319
onwards, they seem not to have lived there during the
period of the Border Wars.   Only when that rough
school of heroism and romance was about to be closed
for ever we find, at the end of Elizabeth's reign, the
' Greys of Howick ' setting up as a distinct local branch.

When George III came to the throne these Greys
of Howick were a numerous clan.   The eldest, Sir
Henry, uncle to the Reform Bill Premier, lived as a
bachelor in the old peel tower of Howick, near the
sea, perhaps already meditating the more habitable
mansion that twenty years later he built in a fortunate
hour.   The only one of Sir Henry's brothers who concerns
our story was Charles Grey the elder, who had already
been wounded at Minden, and was destined to notable
military services in another hemisphere, which earned
him in the end the title of first Earl Grey of Howick.
But he always lived, as a cadet of the family, not at
Howick, but five miles off at Fallodon, a small country
house half-way between the moors and the sea, which
his mother had brought into the Grey inheritance.
Here, on March 13, 1764, his son Charles, the future
Reform Bill Premier, was born, and not many weeks
later, by the death of a baby brother, became the eldest
of his generation.[1]

[1] See genealogical tree at end of book.

SIR HENRY GREY, of Howick, Bart., 1722-1808.
Uncle of the Prime Minister.

From a picture at Howick.

Both Fallodon, his parents' house, where he was born, and Howick, his uncle's house, which he himself was to inhabit for the last forty-four years of his life, were familiar ground to him in his childhood, and in his schoolboy holidays. Fallodon and Howick both breathe the spell of that windy land between hills and sea, which few cast off if they have been bred in it, least of all the Greys in the cherished intervals between one bout of public service and the next. But it was Howick that most won the heart of Charles Grey the younger. It stands, drawn back a mile from the shore, between the lonely ruins of Dunstanborough and the little port of Alnmouth. That coast, since celebrated by Turner and by Swinburne, was then bleakly unknown to good society, which had not yet developed a taste for such severe and distant joys. Their friends in London thought of the Greys, as old Chaucer thought of Alan de Strother, as coming from some place

'Fer in the North, I can not tellé where.'

It would have been happier for Grey if yet more of his boyhood had been passed in the kindly North. But the custom of the age prevailed even with the most loving of parents, and at six years old he was sent to an ill-chosen school at Marylebone. There he remained miserably for three years, suffering from a series of illnesses. The first of these overtook him immediately after his arrival in the South, and the poor little sick child, separated by four long days' posting from his parents' care, was put in the sole charge of a nurse who lived, as luck would have it, at Tyburn. The first day when the boy of six was well enough to be taken out of doors she took him across the road to see a batch of Jews hung for forgery, and lest he should miss any of the sight mounted him on the shoulders of a grenadier. The dying contortions of the wretches as they were one by one turned off the cart, left such an impress on a mind more than ordinarily sensitive that, in the reign of Victoria, the statesman who had passed the Reform Bill would wake sweating from a nightmare vision of this old horror of Hogarth's London.

At nine years old he was sent to Eton, and remained there till he was seventeen (1773–1781). It was here that he first touched the great world of politics and fashion, to which Eton was then an antechamber. Here he began a friendship of more than sixty years' duration with Richard, afterwards Marquis Wellesley, the half-ally of his later political life ; here he formed a yet closer personal attachment with his more short-lived brother Liberals, Sam Whitbread and William Lambton.[1] Canning was such a small boy when Grey left the school that we can hardly suppose that they had yet found occasion to dislike one another.

Grey, I believe, gained much from Eton, but, at the risk of alienating from him a powerful body of opinion, I must confess that he was not a good 'Old Etonian.' In the first year of his Reform Ministry he wrote to Wellesley on July 22, 1831, 'I am to be at Windsor on Sunday for [Eton] Speeches on Monday, where I have not been since I spoke myself fifty years ago.' He refused to send any of his numerous sons to a public school, on the ground that he himself had been taught nothing at the most famous of those establishments. This must be taken as a criticism directed at the limited aims of the curriculum and of the system, for he certainly got the best that Eton set out to provide. He succeeded there, socially and scholastically, and in those days athletic prowess was not indispensable.

Some of Grey's school verses won a place in the

---

[1] Grey was in the Sixth Form 1780–1 ; Wellesley in 1778 ; Whitbread in 1779–80 ; Lambton in 1782.

famous selection published some years later under the
title ' Musae Etonenses.' Although, to judge by his
strictures on the school course, he did not regard the
writing of Latin verse as affording by itself a complete
education, he was nevertheless much devoted to the
lore of that peculiar art, which Milton did not disdain.
In 1842 the octogenarian Marquis of Wellesley sent a
volume containing his own Latin verses to Earl Grey,
aged seventy-eight. The ex-Premier replied to the ex-
Governor-General of India : ' I remember well admiring
when at Eton the beautiful exercises which are contained in this collection, and which then made so great
an impression on me that I could still repeat many of
them by heart.' When we remember what had happened
in the world in East and West during the sixty and odd
years that Grey was carrying about Wellesley's Eton
verses in his head, and what parts the two boys had
played in preserving the *Imperium et Libertas* of modern
Rome, we may think that the schoolrooms as well as
the playing fields of Eton have had their part in English
history.

The fact is that the Eton and Harrow education
of that time was well directed towards a definite if in-
sufficient end. It may have ill served some of the larger
purposes of the community, but at least it forwarded the
success in later life of the most important boys, those
namely who were born to the purple of a seat in either
House of Parliament, or who seemed likely by their
talents to become recipients of a well-bestowed interest
in a rotten borough. As Mr. Butler has admirably
put it,[1] the system of these schools

aimed at the training of statesmen, at a time when statesmanship
consisted largely in winning and retaining the confidence of an
assembly of some six hundred gentlemen. Special attention was
therefore paid to oratory, and oratory of a particular type—
large, dignified, lofty, appealing to the sense of honour and

[1] *Passing of the Great Reform Bill*, J. R. Butler, p. 233.

responsibility of a particular class.   Such was the object of the
Speech-days so much in vogue, not less than of the specialized
study of the Classics as the model of language and taste.   Parliamentary eloquence was founded on the pure and lordly speech
of the ancient poets and orators, who were freely quoted in the
ordinary conversation of gentlemen ; Shakespeare was their only
rival, but he was known with a thoroughness that would be
rare to-day.   Similarity of education combined with similarity
of social position to produce a close society favourable to high
spirit and intensity of life rather than to breadth of sympathy.
For effective debate it is necessary that speakers and audience
should share a common fund of experience and a common *hinter-
land* of thought.

Eton was a recruiting ground for Parliament, not
only because of its peculiar education, but by reason of
its personal connections.   An ' Eton reputation ' was a
long step towards a seat in the House.   Grey might or
might not have sat for Northumberland at twenty-two
if he had never been at Eton, but it is in the highest
degree unlikely that the friends and relations of the
bourgeois Canning and Whitbread would have put those
young gentlemen into the House so soon as they did,
if Eton had not first proclaimed them as two of her
chosen spirits.

It is indeed easy to point out the shortcomings of
an education which Grey himself thought bad.   And
certainly, when the two Houses of public-schoolmen
and classical scholars were asked by an untimely Fate
to deal with the economic and social problems of the
Industrial Revolution during a twenty years' war, the
result for the community was as disastrous as might
have been expected.   But during the greater part of
the eighteenth century, itself a ' classical ' period of
stationary happiness for a considerable portion of the
people of England, this close literary education had at
least the merit of producing an aristocracy fit to set
the fashion to other classes.   Men of the world, but
by no means ashamed of the things of the mind—

brought up to be proud of their knowledge of the Classics, Shakespeare, and Milton, and the histories of Greece, Rome, and Stuart England—the small group of families who governed the State with perhaps indifferent success, proved the best patrons of literature since the Athenian democracy. These aristocrats made the world, that doffed its hat to them, doff to the Muses also. For instance, while Grey was at Eton, the first volumes of Gibbon's History appeared ; at the high prices of that time they only sold 2,000 copies in the first year, but those copies, having been sold to the right kind of people, at once ensured to Gibbon an European reputation, and placed him, in the just regard of his contemporaries, by the side of Livy and Tacitus. Similarly, the great world of fashion and politics imposed on England the worship of Shakespeare ; it is due to the patrons of Garrick and Dr. Johnson that we still call the Elizabethan age, ' the age of Shakespeare,' as if letters were three parts of life. It was in this limited but truly civilised state of society and intellect, now very barely imaginable to us, that Grey was brought up, both at Eton and at home.

While his son was at Eton, General Charles Grey was earning fame as one of the best of our Generals in the war of the American Revolution. In a night onslaught at Paoli, near Valley Forge, he achieved all the conditions of successful surprise, and beat up Wayne's quarters with the cold steel. Among other expedients, he had caused the men whose muskets were loaded to knock out the flints, so as to prevent any chance explosion, a device which gained for the victor of Paoli the honourable nickname of ' no-flint Grey.' During the nineteenth century a portrait of Benjamin Franklin looked down from over the chimney-piece of Howick library at the domestic felicity of the Whig statesmen descended from this fine Tory soldier. When the British troops occupied Philadelphia, the portrait had been taken out of Franklin's house as the only permissible spoils of war, implying indeed a compliment to the worldwide fame of the philosophic rebel. The plunderer was no less interesting a person than the unfortunate Major André, then General Grey's aide-de-camp, who presented the picture to his chief. In the twentieth century Albert Earl Grey, Governor-General of Canada, gave back the portrait to the American people, who presented him instead with an excellent copy that now hangs in the same place at Howick.

In 1781 Grey left Eton for Trinity College, Cambridge. The eighteenth century was not a time of profound learning or of intellectual ferment at either University. The dons, as described by Gibbon for Oxford, and by Wordsworth for Cambridge, seem scarcely to have been libelled in Rowlandson's caricatures. They were little better than the other clerical sinecurists of that epoch, with some touch of eccentricity often added to distinguish the academician. On the walls of Trinity College there is a strange absence of portraits of great men of learning between Bentley and Porson. One must look before or after the sleepy century for true academic fame. Under such careless tutelage young men of family at least enjoyed themselves, continuing the lazy, lively existence, far from purely philistine, which they had begun at Eton or at Westminster.

Grey [1] consorted at Cambridge with his Eton friends, Lambton, of his own College, and the Johnian

---

[1] The *Dictionary of National Biography* incorrectly states that he was at King's, no doubt because he came so prominently from Eton. His real College is stated not only in a MS. by his son, but in Mr. Rouse Ball's monumental work, *Trinity College Admissions*, where we read, under the year 1781 :—' Grey, Charles, son of Charles Grey of Falladon (query Fallowdon), Northumberland. School, Eton (Mr. Davies). Age 17. Fellow-commoner, Nov. 12, 1781. Tutors, Mr. Therond and Mr. Cranke. Matriculated 1781. Did not graduate.' The Trinity registrar of that date was probably not the first, and certainly he was not the last, to boggle over the spelling of Fallodon.

CHARLES GREY at the time he left Eton.

From the picture by Romney at Howick.

Whitbread. It may have been in their company that he first developed a leaning towards what we now call Liberal opinions, which were a novelty in his father's house. At any rate, when the test of the French Revolution came, ten years later, this Eton and Cambridge trio figured together in the list, once of reproach, now of honour, of the Society of ' Friends of the People,' and stood together in Parliament for the down-trodden liberties of Englishmen till the death of Lambton in 1797 and of Whitbread in 1815. The brewer married Grey's sister ; and Lambton, the landed magnate of County Durham, was the father of Grey's son-in-law and Cabinet colleague, the famous Lord Durham of the Canadian report. During their Cambridge period the three friends were painted by Romney, each seated with a book in his hand, as if the three pictures formed one set ; they were done for the Head Master of Eton as ' leaving presents,' and hang in the Provost's Lodge with other fine portraits by Reynolds and Romney of the young men whom Eton delighted to honour.[1]

But it would be a mistake to imagine that these three scholars and future statesmen chose while at Cambridge ' to scorn delights and live laborious days,' like Pitt at Pembroke a few years before. They were devoted friends of the Falstaff of the University, Thomas Adkin of Corpus, a Bachelor of Arts, a little older than themselves, whose strange life and ready humour have been rescued from oblivion by Gunning. In his quarters at the White Bear Inn, known in his day as ' Adkin College,' nearly opposite Trinity, he used to entertain Grey and his other friends with Attic revelry, where much true wit degenerated, as night wore on, into Bacchanalian riot.

---

[1] For reproductions see Mr. Lionel Cust's *Eton Portraits*. The reproduction opposite is from the replica at Howick, where it forms one of a set of Romneys representing the four sons of General Grey.

Whenever the Proctors entered the Inn [writes Gunning] for the purpose of sending to their respective Colleges any undergraduates who might be found amongst so tumultuous an assemblage, they were immediately informed by the waiter that the noise proceeded from a private room where *Squire Adkin* was giving a dinner to a few friends. Whether this was a sufficient answer to prevent the University officers entering the room, I am not able to say, *as the experiment was never made* ; but the waiters were always questioned as to there being any undergraduates in the party. They never failed to answer, they could not tell, but imagined there were none, as they had seen neither caps nor gowns, and that the gentlemen were all in boots and leather breeches.[1]

The studies of Cambridge were in those days in somewhat too striking contrast to the rigorous classicism of Eton. The only letter of Grey's of this period that has survived, written in his second term at Trinity, says :

You enquire how I like Cambridge. I answer, very much. My only objection to it is that I think the study too confined. If a man is not a mathematician he is nobody. Mathematicks and Philosophy supply the place of Classicks and all other studies ; though whatever mode is most agreeable to a young man he is at perfect liberty to pursue.

After school and college came, in those days, the third part of a gentleman's education—the Grand Tour. Foreign travel was then taken, not as now in sips periodically administered once or twice a year, but in one deep draught in early youth. During most of the time between his departure from Trinity in 1784 and the beginning of his Parliamentary career in 1787, Grey was moving about through Southern France, Switzerland, and Italy, at first alone and later ' in the suite of Henry Duke of Cumberland.' One long letter of his, that chance has preserved, gives us a glimpse of him,

---

[1] Gunning's *Cambridge*, i. 56–66 ; Broughton (Hobhouse), *Recollections*, i. 92.

like so many before and after, fascinated by Palladio's
Theatre at Vicenza, astonished by the Roman amphi-
theatre at Verona, depressed by the gloom of Mantua,
and preferring the scenery of Lago Maggiore even to
the shores of Lake Leman. In the larger cities he had
the opportunity of seeing much of foreign society, for
travelling Englishmen then enjoyed the hospitality not
only of the French but of the Italian Courts and salons.
He came away with a lifelong skill in the language and
literature of Italy. The Grand Tour helped to develop
in him that excellent habit of mind whereby he always
regarded foreign countries, not as pawns in the diplo-
matic game, but as places inhabited by human beings
with rights and aspirations of their own.

In July 1786, while still abroad, he was returned
at a by-election for the County of Northumberland, and
he first took his seat in the new session of January 1787.
The scarcity of family papers prior to 1792 makes it
impossible to analyse with certainty the motives of his
early political attachments. The difficulty is the greater
because these motives, before the issues raised by the
French Revolution sobered him for life, were probably
not a little personal, and as much connected with
Brooks's Club, Devonshire House, and the company
of Charles Fox and his friends, as with any principle
in politics. It is indeed hard to discern any principle,
least of all of a Liberal character, in the actions of
Opposition during the years when they were denouncing Pitt's Free Trade and pacific policy towards France,
and plotting to climb back to power on the shoulders
of the Prince Regent. Grey's father was, if anything,
a supporter of Pitt, and the junior member for
Northumberland had been returned at his first election
with that delightful freedom from pledges and obliga-
tions which county members then so often enjoyed.
Even after he had been taking a leading part in opposition for several months, Fox still denied to him the

title of 'party man.' [1]   But it would appear that from
the moment he arrived in London he had gravitated
to the society of those who were working for Pitt's
overthrow.   And, indeed, for good company and good
talk, no party was ever better worth joining than that
of Fox, Burke, Sheridan, and the authors of the *Rolliad*
when it was still swelling in size at every new edition.
Grey had soon adopted all the quarrels of his allies
with the light-hearted enthusiasm of two-and-twenty.

The only account of Grey's choice of a party which
has come down to us are the words which the famous
Lady Holland, then Lady Webster, wrote at the end
of 1793.   They presumably represent some real tradition on the subject, but it must be remembered that
they were written seven years after the events related,
and at a period when the writer was not yet in the
heart of the Whig circle, and had at most but a slight
acquaintance with Grey.   The first sentence sounds
absurd to those who know anything about the later
Grey, but may well have been less untrue about his
early youth :

Grey is a man of violent temper and unbounded ambition.
His connections were Ministerial, but on his return from abroad
both parties entertained hopes of him.   His uncle, Sir Harry
[of Howick], is a rich, old, positive, singular man, leads a retired
life, but was always eager upon politics, particularly against the
Coalition—an infamous thing, by-the-bye.   His father, Sir
Charles Grey, is attached to Government as a military man,
and is intimately connected with Colonel Barré and Lord Lans-
down, who at that time supported the Ministry.   Grey was
elected whilst abroad, therefore not pledged to any particular

---

[1] 'Mr. Fox replied to what Mr. Pitt had said of Mr. Grey's being
a party man, and declared that the hon. gentleman was not of that
description, but he hoped by degrees he might become a party man'
(*Hansard*, xxvi. 1198, May 28, 1787).   In a letter of 1782, at the
age of 18, Grey had spoken with pleasure of the advent of the Rockingham
ministry to power ; so he had not been, even at that early age, an adherent
of George III and Lord North.

party. The fashion was to be in Opposition ; the Prince of Wales belonged to it, and he then was not disliked ; all the beauty and wit of London were on that side, and the seduction of Devonshire House prevailed. Besides, Pitt's manner displeased him on his first speech, whereas Fox was all conciliation and encouragement.[1]

In view of the future, it was lucky that Grey fell under the influence of Fox. But in 1787 there was little reason for a Reformer to prefer Opposition to Government. The Rockingham or Foxite Whigs had delivered the country from North and the ' King's Friends ' in 1782, put an end to the personal government of the Crown, and taken the first step, in Burke's Economic Reform Bill, towards the purification of English politics. But they then proceeded to deprive themselves, by a series of amazing blunders, of the opportunity to do any more good. When Rockingham died, Fox and Shelburne quarrelled, from incompatibility of temperament rather than on any public ground. To make good the loss of Shelburne's party, Fox entered into coalition with North. That easy-going nobleman, who had lost America rather than hurt George III's feelings, was still hated by that great majority of his fellow-countrymen who did not know by personal contact what a good-natured man he was. The coalition not only shocked the moral sense of the ordinary citizen, but alienated from the Whigs the one progressive element of that day, the Yorkshire Parliamentary Reformers led by Wyvill, who leaned for some years to come on the broken reed of Pitt's Liberal inclinations. The King, rising to his opportunity of revenge, tripped up the heels of his Ministers over their India Bill. Fox made mistake after mistake, and Pitt, the unerring tactician, soon established himself in the confidence of his countrymen, and began his long reign as Prime Minister. The King's personal rule was not restored, but

[1] *The Journal of Elizabeth, Lady Holland*, 1908, i. 100.

George III unfortunately retained in practice a veto on all great Liberal measures—Parliamentary Reform, Catholic Emancipation, and Abolition of Slave Trade. That power of veto was largely due to the weakness of Pitt, whose worst fault was unwillingness to risk a fall in order to pass the measures which he knew to be right, and who, as his friend Wilberforce learned bitterly to lament, preferred to govern the country by ' influence ' instead of by ' principle.' [1]   But at least he could govern.   In the ten years between the war of the American and the war of the French Revolution the country rose, in prosperity and in prestige, from the degradation to which George III had reduced it.   The wits of Brooks's jested about Pitt's youth.   But in fact he was prematurely old in spirit—cautious, dignified, formidable, experienced, laborious, wise ; but with a mind that, after a splendid springtime, too soon became closed to generous enthusiasms and new ideas, and ceased to understand human nature save as it is known to a shrewd and cynical Government Whip.   He was still being twitted as ' the schoolboy ' when he had acquired all the characteristics of the schoolmaster. While Fox always retained the faults and merits of youth, Pitt early acquired those of old age.

Pitt, in his studious years at Cambridge, had mastered the new doctrines of Adam Smith, and very shortly afterwards he was putting them into practice in his budgets.   It is true that his early Free Trade work was soon undone by the war taxation imposed by himself and his successors, and his *rapprochement* with France by the Commercial Treaty was the prelude to a twenty years' war.   But, shortlived as it proved to be, the Commercial Treaty of 1787 was, as Mr. Lecky says, ' probably the most valuable result of the legis-lation of Pitt.'   It was an admirable measure, both

---

[1] *Private Papers of W. Wilberforce*, Unwin, 1897, pp. 72-4.   A most remarkable passage.

commercially and as a means of putting an end to the
traditional antagonism of England and France. The
arguments of Opposition were directed, not so much
against the commercial principles involved, on which
Brooks's had no very clearly defined ideas, as against
the political issue of improved relations with France.
In so far as this criticism was more than factious, it
was out of date. The traditional Whig hostility to the
despotic and persecuting House of Bourbon had come
down from William III through Chatham to Fox and
Grey. But in 1787 the character of the French Monarchy, already staggering to its doom, was very different
from what it had been in the time of the Dragonnades.[1]

On February 21, 1787, Grey rose to make his
maiden speech against the Commercial Treaty. ' French
perfidy ' was his theme, and the young orator could not
refrain from ' *Timeo Danaos*.' But it was a fine speech,
and on the strength of it the House of Commons, then
at the highwater-mark of its oratorical and debating
genius, accepted the tyro as one of its leading men.

A new speaker [so Addington wrote to his father] presented
himself to the House, and went through his first performance
with an éclat which has not been equalled to my recollection.
His name is Grey. He is not more than twenty-two years of
age ; and he took his seat only in the present session. I do not
go too far in declaring that in the advantage of figure, voice,
elocution, and manner, he is not surpassed by any member of the
House ; and I grieve to say that he was last night in the ranks of
Opposition, from whence there is no chance of his being detached.

Thus, by a brilliant piece of invective on the wrong
side of a question that he did not understand, the young
man from Northumberland at twenty-two years of age

---

[1] On the fall of the Bastille, July 1789, Fox declares that ' all my
prepossessions against French connections for this country will be at
an end, and most part of my European system of politics will be altered,'
if France ceases to be an absolutist Power. But the revolution that
at once made Fox friendly to France, ere long made Pitt hostile.

became one of the most envied in that most enviable of all the aristocracies of history, the men and women who look out from the canvasses of Reynolds and Romney with a divine self-satisfaction, bred of unchallenged possession of all that was really best in a great civilisation, in the years when Rousseau was no more than a theory and Voltaire was still a fashion.

It is clear from Addington's letter that not a little of Grey's first success as an orator [1] was due to his appearance, to his manner, and to the general effect of his delivery. He was a handsome man. In the middle period of Grey's life, no less a judge than Byron spoke of ' his patrician thoroughbred look that I dote on.' In his old age, the Reform Premier is the most graceful figure among his colleagues in ' H. B.'s ' lifelike cartoons. In early youth, though many thought him ' supercilious,' he had, when he wished, the gift to please ; and before the domesticated period of his life began in 1794, he achieved successes such as fell to few in that world of *fin-de-siècle* gallantry. The men and women among whom he moved when he first came to London lacked both the virtues and the vices of the austere. They felt themselves above the censure of any class but their own, and they had not yet been frightened by the French Revolution or reclaimed by the Evangelical movement. But these days of unchartered freedom were already numbered. The change from the high society that Fox led to that of the generation which ostracised Byron, is an English version of the change from the Renaissance Courts of the early Cinquecento to the Italy of the Jesuit reaction.

[1] In a book of little value that belonged to Lord Macaulay occur the words, ' No member of either house of the British Parliament will be ranked amongst the orators of this country, *whom Lord North did not see*, or who did not see Lord North.' Macaulay has underscored the words here printed in italics, and written on the margin ' Lord North, poor man, was blind when Lord Grey came into Parliament.'

Within a few weeks of his entry into the House of Commons, his social success and his prominence in the Whig world had won him the always fatal privilege of intimacy with George, Prince of Wales. It is difficult to say whether the ladies or the statesmen who put their trust in that Prince fared the worst, though both ladies and statesmen courted their own discredit. In his youth he was the bane and disgrace of the Whigs, and in his old age of the Tories. And in each case the worst trouble arose from his conduct towards a wife.

The original connection of the Prince of Wales with the Whigs was due in part to his lively and dissolute manners, which fitted in better with Fox's and Sheridan's ideas of good company than with those of Pitt. There was also the natural tendency of an Opposition in disgrace at Court to fall back on the Heir Apparent ; Fox and the Prince of Wales both hated George III, and were hated by him. If and when the Prince of Wales became Regent or King, he could dismiss Pitt and call in Fox. Such action would probably create a Whig Parliamentary majority ; for, although the ' King's friends ' as such had disappeared from politics, it was calculated that some 185 members of the House of Commons were always ready to vote for any Government actually in power, if it was not peculiarly unpopular.[1] This calculation underlies the political history of the whole period.

So the Whigs shared the Carlton House revels, and championed the national payment of the Carlton House debts. This was bad, but there was worse to come. The Prince was passionately in love with Mrs. Fitzherbert, a Roman Catholic lady, at that time a widow. She would not yield to his wishes unless he married her. But even marriage was open to two objections— first, that if the Prince married a Roman Catholic he was liable to forfeit the succession to the Crown ; and

---

[1] *England under the Hanoverians,* Grant Robertson, p. 324, note.

second, that by the Royal Marriage Act he could not until he was twenty-five contract a legal union without the King's consent. Fox, in a letter of December 10, 1785, laid these considerations before the Prince, and urged him in the strongest terms 'not to think of marriage till you can marry legally. A mock marriage, for it can be no other, is neither honourable for any of the parties, nor, with respect to your Royal Highness, even safe.'

To this the Prince replied, on the next day :

Make yourself easy, my dear friend. Believe me the world will now soon be convinced that there not only is, but never was, any ground for these reports which of late have been so malevolently circulated.

Four days later [1] he secretly married Mrs. Fitzherbert. His arrangements for the marriage must have been far advanced when he wrote to his 'dear friend' to induce him to believe that no such step would be taken.

As the King's consent had not been obtained, the union was not legal ; indeed, the Prince subsequently married another wife while Mrs. Fitzherbert was still alive. But since her Church recognised the ceremony as valid, Mrs. Fitzherbert chose to regard it as sufficient safeguard for her honour. Since the publication of the fact would endanger the Prince's succession to the Crown, she always observed a magnanimous silence. Her reticence and her sufferings atone for her mistake in consenting to a ceremony on terms so doubtful for herself and so dangerous for her husband.

More than a year later, at the end of April, 1787, the Prince, supported by the Whigs, was trying to get the Carlton House debts paid off by the nation. While the question was at issue, the Tory member Rolle, the exasperated hero of the *Rolliad*, raised in the House the rumour that the Prince was married to a Roman

---

[1] The marriage was on December 15, 1785, not, as has often been stated, on the 21st. See Wilkins, *Mrs. Fitzherbert*, i. 99.

it in Gladstonian language. The Opposition for once was popular, since it resisted an adventure which interested but few people in our island. Grey took a leading part in the debates, and now acquired his profound hostility to the Turkish dominion in Europe, which served Greece well in 1830.[1] From this time forward till the end of his life Grey stands also as a firm advocate of peace. Of the eight resolutions that he moved on April 12, 1791, the first was : ' That it is at all times, and particularly under the present circumstances, the interest of this country to preserve peace.' He declared that to fight about Ocksakow was an abuse of the theory of the ' Balance of Power.'

Now that France has become no longer formidable, a rival is discovered in a corner of Europe. We are now to contend for forts on the Black Sea, as if we were fighting for our hearths and altars. This is a source of affliction to the peasant, and those who propose to lay new burdens on him for that purpose add insult to oppression.

The arguments are almost precisely those of John Bright in opposing the Crimean War, which is in turn defended on much the same grounds as Pitt's proposed interference about Ocksakow. In this speech of Grey's we seem to see the guiding principles of his life beginning to emerge out of the chaotic ambitions and partisanships of his early years.

[1] See pp. 227–230, below.

CHAPTER II

THE FRIENDS OF THE PEOPLE

The trumpet of Liberty sounds through the world,
    And the Universe starts at the sound ;
Her standard Philosophy's hand has unfurled,
    And the nations are thronging around.

> *Chorus :* Fall, tyrants ! fall ! fall ! fall !
>   These are the days of liberty !
>   Fall, tyrants, fall !

Proud castles of despotism, dungeons and cells,
    The tempest shall sweep you away.
From the east to the west the dread hurricane swells,
    And the tyrants are filled with dismay.

Poor vassals who crawl by the Vistula's stream,
    Hear ! hear the glad call and obey !
Rise, nations ! who worship the sun and the beams,
    And drive your Pizarros away.

Shall Britons the chorus of Liberty hear
    With a cold and insensible mind ?
No—the triumphs of freedom each Briton shall hear,
    And contend for the rights of mankind.

(*Written by Mr. John Taylor of Norwich, and first sung at the famous Whig banquet at Holkham given by Coke of Norfolk to celebrate the centenary of the English Revolution, Nov. 5, 1788.*)

DURING the years immediately preceding the French Revolution, Pitt's enemies are too often found standing for no principle higher than factious opposition. But ' the times that try men's souls ' were now to prove that the Whig party was still the seed-bed of principles that contained the future ; while the forces on which Pitt depended for power had, when brought to the test, no thought or help for the new era, struggling to be born, except dull resistance to all change. As soon as the French Revolution and the democratic movement that answered to it in this island had made the issues real, the Tory party was found to be solid in favour of repressive measures and against Parliamentary Reform. The Whigs were divided, but owing mainly to Fox, and not a little to Grey, the nucleus of the party was secured for the cause of progress. It was Portland and the Burkite Whigs who seceded and merged their identity in the Tory ranks ; while the fifty M.P.'s and half-dozen peers who stood, disarmed and apparently helpless, beneath Fox's tattered banner, were constituting the party destined to reform England and govern her during the best half of the coming century. Their action, though it appeared to many then, and appears to some now, as unpatriotic and seditious, laid down the lines of modern politics in our island, and provided a Parliamentary channel through which the democratic ferment going on underground could in the end rise to the surface without a convulsion fatal to the commonwealth. The story of the anti-Jacobin and democratic movements of the 'nineties, and the position of the Foxite Whigs in relation to the two, is of greater interest than any part of our later political history until the Reform Bill itself. In the last decade of the eighteenth century, the times, if tragic, were great, and the leaders on each side, though far from impeccable, had the genius and the manhood to play great parts in the great manner.

Why was it that half the Whigs, in spite of the ' aristocratic ' character of their party, stood for liberty and enfranchisement when the rest of the upper classes were seized by a reactionary panic ? There was a soul in the Whig party that Carlton House could degrade but could not kill ; it was alive even during the winter of the Regency debates. That soul was an idealised and traditional love of liberty. Coleridge was surprised that so aristocratic a lady as Georgiana, Duchess of Devonshire, should write verses to celebrate William Tell's defiance of the tyrant.

> O Lady, nursed in pomp and pleasure !
> Whence learn'd you that heroic measure ?

So the poet asked. The true answer would have been that the Duchess was bred in the Whig tradition, which fostered an ideal passion for the overthrow of tyrants.

The tradition of the party started from the solid achievement of the destruction of Stuart despotism. This, to the Whigs, was the central event of history. They seem to have regarded Hampden as the first Whig, and Milton as the party laureate. Cromwell was still ' a fiend hid in a cloud ' : the deed for which they were constrained to condemn him was yet his dark title to glory. He had ' ga'ed Kings to ken they had a crick in their neck.' Whig tradition, so confident on other subjects, never quite knew what to make of Oliver. It was a relief to turn to the Revolution of 1688, and to celebrate that.

During the long, corrupting domination of the party in the days of Walpole and his successors, the Whig soul nearly died of fatness. But it was purified and revived in the uphill battle against George III, by the moral and intellectual splendour of Burke, and by sympathy with the American Revolution. Whiggism began to take on a less insular form, partly from the act of looking across the Atlantic, partly under the influence of the cosmopolitan ' Philosophy ' of that era. Yet it always remained an unique British product. Its religious toleration and dislike of ' priestcraft ' is Locke's or Priestley's, not Voltaire's. Vague modern hopes of liberty for all mankind blend with a hearty English pride in ourselves, as the pioneers who had long ago hewn out the path still to be traversed by less favoured

nations. When, in November 1788, the centenary of
the British Revolution was celebrated by the party
whose chief asset was that somewhat too immortal
memory, the younger Whigs were generously stirred
by the prologue to the French Revolution then enacting
across the Channel. In accepting the invitation to the
Centenary banquet at Holkham, Windham writes to
Coke, ' a festival to celebrate the Revolution is a proper
reception for a person just come from France.'[1]

It was at this banquet that the song, ' Fall, tyrants,
fall ! ' was first sung.[2] The words, with their pathetic
faith in the near future of mankind, perpetuate that
fleeting hour of exaltation, when the traditions of the
Whig party and the aspirations of the age of enlightenment seemed about to be realised together, first in
France and then over all the world. Such were the
ideas, or rather the ideals, which prepared the minds
of Fox and Grey to sympathise with the French Revolution, to demand civic rights for Dissenters and Roman
Catholics, to protect free speech and free association,
and to support the movement for Parliamentary Reform
even when it assumed the novel shape of a claim put
forward by the working men.

The agitation for Parliamentary Reform in the last
quarter of the eighteenth century falls into three periods,
under the leadership of three distinct classes. First,
there is the movement of the Yorkshire Freeholders,
patronised by half the Whig party, which culminated
in Pitt's Reform Bill of 1785 and declined after its
rejection. Secondly, there is the movement led by the
philosophic Dissenters, which we may call the ' Bastille'
movement ; it was crushed by the Birmingham riots of
1791. The third movement was that of the working

---

[1] Oct. 18, 1788. *Coke of Norfolk*, p. 217. Windham at this
time was what he himself would afterwards have called ' a Jacobin.'
[2] Printed at head of this chapter.

men of industrial London and the provinces, inspired by Paine, organised by Hardy in 1792, and forcibly suppressed by Pitt in the next half-dozen years. Contemporary with this last and most significant phase is the Parliamentary Whig movement led by Grey, protected by Fox, and organised in the short-lived but important Society of the Friends of the People.

The original Reform movement of the Yorkshire Freeholders had been Old English in its aims and methods. It was not cosmopolitan in its outlook ; nor was it ' democratic ' in the modern use of the word, for the economic changes of the Industrial Revolution had not then created the ' democracy ' that we know. It was an union under Whig aristocratic patronage of those old-fashioned ' freeholders,' the middle classes of town and country, who had beaten the Stuart Kings. They demanded Parliamentary Reform, not with a general view of elevating the lower class or of enriching the poor, but to attain good government for the nation as a whole. The movement had, in fact, been provoked by George III, and was intended to put an end to his personal rule exercised through the nominated and bribed majority of the House of Commons. The object was to restore the old English constitution, corrupted by time and evil counsellors.

It was almost as much a movement of occasion as of principle. When, therefore, the rule of the ' King's Friends ' came to an end, after 1782, and when the disasters and miseries of the American war were being repaired by the healing policy of Pitt as peace Minister, the agitation lost so much of its force that Pitt threw it over, after a half-hearted attempt at a Reform Bill in 1785. Wyvill and Major Cartwright, deeply disappointed by Pitt's desertion and by the collapse of their once powerful movement, survived to attach themselves to the more democratic aspirations of the coming epoch.

The second era of the Reform movement covers

the years immediately preceding and following the fall of the Bastille. The leadership lies with the philosophic Dissenters, Price and Priestley. Pitt not only dropped Parliamentary Reform, but in 1787, and again in 1789, he opposed the abolition of the Test and Corporation Acts which debarred Dissenters and Roman Catholics from civil rights. Fox, on the other hand, warmly espoused the cause of religious freedom, and asserted the modern principle that 'religion is not a proper test for a political institution.' In these Test Act debates, which precede the French Revolution, we have the first clear indication that Fox was capable of founding modern Liberalism, and Pitt that extravagant Toryism that was killed by the Reform Bill.

The leading Dissenters, now hopeless of relief from Pitt or from the existing House of Commons, began to agitate for Parliamentary Reform as a step necessary to their own civil enfranchisement. Dissenters and Parliamentary Reformers alike were alienated from Pitt and, in spite of the unsavoury memories of the Coalition and of the Regency debates, began with caution to draw towards Fox and the more liberal section of the Whigs. In this juncture of our affairs, the news from France began to affect the political imagination of Englishmen. France, not yet drenched with blood, had replaced a despotism by a constitutional monarchy, and was framing a code of laws which put men of every creed on the same platform of civil rights. The more progressive members of the Whig party, including Fox and Grey, were at one with the philosophic Dissenters in acclaiming the dawn of world-wide political enfranchisement and religious equality, while Burke, who already heard the fall of civilisation in the falling stones of the Bastille, flung himself against Price and the Unitarian Reformers with all the heaviest weapons of his splendid armoury.

Burke's 'Reflections on the French Revolution' (Nov. 1790), whatever its author may have intended, appealed

D

to passions only less cruel, and certainly more unpro-
voked, than those which he justly execrated in the
French mob.   It was an angel's trumpet, but it roused
the fiends.

An unreasoned hatred of Dissenters, common in
the higher orders of society and locally in the slum
population, was stirred to fury as the result direct and
indirect of the writings of Burke, who also denounced
the Parliamentary Reformers and friends of the French
Revolution.   In the long battle between Reformers and
anti-Reformers, that began with the Birmingham riots of
1791 and ended with the passing of Lord Grey's Reform
Bill, the combatants drew much of their devotion and most
of their cruelty from sectarian zeal—except in Scotland,
where the fires of political hatred could be thrice heated
without the bellows of religion.   The more we study
the local details of this forty years' war over which Grey
spent his life so loftily presiding, the more does the
sectarian aspect emerge.   For example, the volumes in
the British Museum of the correspondence of Reeves'
'Loyal' Association of 1792 reveal how largely the
Reform movement in particular towns and villages was
an effort of Dissenters, and how much the counteracting
'loyalist' movement was set on foot by churchmen and
clergymen, in a panic of the old Dr. Sacheverel type,
intensified by the news from France.   In 1831 we find
the same sectarian cleavage, except that then the Church
clergy were deserted politically by their congregations,
and the mob of Birmingham had gone round *en masse*
to Reform.

The ministers of a State Church have a natural
bent and perhaps an obligation to emphasise the
conservative side of life.   But the degree to which
the Church clergy of that era were conservative is
not easily credible to-day, when so many clergymen
endeavour to see through the eyes of their parishioners
in working-class districts, which their predecessors
contemptuously left to the care of dissenting preachers.

In the sleepy days of the eighteenth century, laymen complacently regarded the parson as the chartered tithe-eater, and he often regarded himself primarily as the possessor of a snug freehold. When the old order began to change, when news came over of Church spoliation in France, and men discussed in alehouses what the community got from the parsons in return for so many tithe-sheaves and tithe-pigs, the clergy took serious alarm, and, as frightened men will do, too often made a virtue of the most unchristian actions against their neighbours. In the earlier age of good-nature and enlightenment, Dr. Johnson's attitude to Dissenters reads as an amusing idiosyncrasy ; when we see the word ' Dissenter ' coming below on the page, we know we are in for sport. But there was nothing amusing in the treatment of Dissenters in town and country during the iron age ushered in by the Birmingham riots of July 1791.

Priestley was a scientist of European reputation in an age when scientists were few. He was a man of blameless life and high public spirit. He was not a Republican, but he was a Dissenter—nay, a Unitarian —and he was now active in favour of Parliamentary Reform and Repeal of the Test Acts, and in public approval of the general course of the French Revolution up to the summer of 1791. Therefore his house and scientific instruments were destroyed by the ' Church and State ' mob of Birmingham, who had been incited against Nonconformists by sermons and pamphlets of the local clergy, and were personally encouraged on the night of riot by two J.P.'s. Dissenting chapels and the private houses of Dissenters as blameless and as unpolitical as the local historian William Hutton, were destroyed, with every appearance of connivance on the part of the Magistrates.[1]

---

[1] The most intimate account of the affair is in the *Life of W. Hutton*, 1816.

This action was hailed with delight by many who should have known better. The men who were rallying to protect 'property' meant only the property of Churchmen, and those who denounced 'the swinish multitude' in the abstract, rejoiced in the mob-law of Birmingham. The Marquis of Buckingham wrote to his brother Lord Grenville, the Foreign Secretary : 'I am not sorry for this excess, excessive as it has been'; and Lord Auckland, the British Ambassador at the Hague, wrote to him in a similar strain. Grenville himself expressed disapproval of the riots, but Pitt said nothing, and voted against Whitbread's motion for enquiry. Fox, with Grey and his Eton friends, Lambton and Whitbread, stood up in vain for justice. The motion for enquiry was lost by 189 votes to 46. In the course of the debate Grey said :

It was not a political, but a religious mob, actuated by the most horrid and sanguinary spirit of bigotry and persecution. Many other houses belonging to persons known to entertain the same religious sentiments with Dr. Priestley were set on fire and destroyed amidst the acclamations of *Church and King for ever ! Down with the Presbyterians !* and the French Revolution appeared plainly to have been not the real cause but merely the pretext of these horrid devastations.

Such was the way in which the most learned and respectable men in England were treated if they happened to be Dissenters and to advocate Parliamentary Reform. The riots took place more than a year before the fall of the French Monarchy and the September massacres, and a year and a half before the outbreak of the war between England and France, which has been pleaded as a sufficient excuse for the whole spirit and system of persecution of Liberal opinions in this epoch. Indeed, more than six months after the Birmingham riots, Pitt declared in the House of Commons that we might 'reasonably expect fifteen years of peace.'

The spirit of religious and political bigotry was

now thoroughly aroused. The authorities, both local and central, smiled on outrage. More orthodox Dissenters were scarcely less obnoxious than Unitarians, and not a few were forced to abandon their business and follow Priestley across the Atlantic.

The second phase of the Reform Movement, as championed by the Dissenters in the palmy days of the fall of the Bastille, may be said to have been put down before the end of 1791. Early in the following year a more significant agitation was begun by a class of men who had never yet acted in politics on their own behalf—the working men in the great towns.

The democratic movement in England—that is to say, the claim put forward by the common people themselves that they should choose their governors in order to improve their own conditions of life—owed its origin to the spectacle of the French Revolution and to the writings of Tom Paine. And the same causes that gave it birth proved in the first instance its undoing. The forcible suppression for so many years of the English movement was rendered possible by the course of the foreign revolution that aroused it, and by the impolitic and uncompromising logic of its first champion.

Paine was an English Quaker by origin. But he had early settled in America, where his pamphlet ' Common Sense ' had done much to persuade the colonists to cut the knot of their difficulties with England by declaring themselves an independent republic. Paine was again in England, and as soon as he read Burke's ' Reflections on the French Revolution ' he sat down to write a reply. The First Part of the ' Rights of Man ' appeared in February 1791.

In answer to Burke's ultra-conservative doctrine, which tended to bind up the English constitution for ever by the pact of 1689, Paine stated the full democratic thesis : that government is derived from the people, can be altered at their will, and must be carried on for their benefit, through a system of popular representation. The pamphlet circulated by tens of thousands among classes who hitherto knew nothing of politics, save when at election time 'the quality' dispensed beer and money to make a mob for the hustings. The idea that politics was an affair of the common people as such, and a means by which they could alleviate their poverty, was new and strange. But the events in France had roused our ancestors to unwonted mental activity, and in 1791-2 Burke and Paine were read and discussed with the simple eagerness natural to men plunged for the first time into political speculation. It was a fine and well-matched debate, in which the mind and character of Englishmen were expanding, certainly not all in one direction. But one of the two protagonists unworthily appealed to have his rival lynched : Burke declared that the proper way to reply to Paine was by 'criminal justice.'

Government, however, declined, in spite of much shrill advice, to prosecute the First Part of the 'Rights of Man,' where the author had not clearly drawn out all the inferences of his representative theory of government. But in the Second Part, published in February 1792, Paine's logical sword came right out of the scabbard. He claimed that all the hereditary elements in the constitution, both Monarchy and House of Lords, ought to be abolished, and the country governed by its representatives alone, sitting either in one or two Chambers. Government would then be carried on for the benefit of the mass of the people. Pensions on the taxes now granted to the rich would be diverted, and used, together with a graduated income-tax, to give education to the poor, old age pensions, and maternity benefit.

Far the greater number of Paine's 'criminal' propositions are accomplished facts of the present day.

The only part of the ' Rights of Man ' that can possibly be called seditious lies in its Republicanism. Yet surely Major Cartwright put the true case, when he said at Horne Tooke's trial that he ' did not consider Paine's writings as a conspiracy to overthrow government, but as discussions on the subject of government.' Paine had not advised conspiracy or rebellion. The country would have sifted out for itself what it wanted in Paine's doctrine and rejected the rest, as indeed it has since done. But the controversy was cut short : the Government prosecuted and suppressed the ' Rights of Man,' and Paine, warned in time by his friend, the poet Blake, fled for his life to France, where he shortly got into trouble by denouncing the Terror and endeavouring to save the life of Louis XVI.

Paine had most rashly identified his theory of representative government with a scheme of rigid Republicanism. For many years to come this confusion continued in the common mind. Even Francis Place, speaking of the workmen's clubs of that era, writes, ' All the leading members of the London Corresponding Society were *Republicans ; that is, they were friendly to a representative form of government*.' This confusion of terms seems ridiculous to us, who are long accustomed to representative government in the form of a constitutional monarchy. But we can understand how the confusion came about, if we examine what was then the practice of the constitution, and what was the theory of it held by Paine's enemies. The royal and aristocratic party in England spoke of the existing constitution as the ' direct contrary ' of democratic or representative. For example, in 1794, Pitt's attorney-general, Sir John Scott, better known by his later title of Lord Eldon, tried to get Thomas Hardy, the founder of the Corresponding Society, condemned to death for high treason on the ground that the object of the Corresponding Society was ' to form a representative government in this country '—' *a representative government, the direct contrary of the government which is established here.'* [1] The forms of our constitution have altered so little since then, that we fail to remember how completely its spirit and practice have changed, and hence we often misjudge the men and controversies of that time.

In advising the English to abolish the form of monarchy, Paine made a ruinous mistake ; he was too much of an American, a theorist, a 'friend of the human race,' and altogether too little of an Englishman to see that his Republican logic would not apply to our island. But the error was not as gratuitous as it would be to-day. Monarchy in the reign of George III was very different from monarchy in the reign of George V. George III had lost us America, and was destined to prevent the reconciliation of Ireland. He stood in the way of the abolition of the slave trade, and of any chance of parliamentary reform. Grey was no Republican, but there was probably a good deal in common between what Grey said in private and what Paine said in public about the powers enjoyed by the inhabitant of Buckingham Palace—' the gentleman at the end of the Mall,' as he was called by the Whigs. [2]

The Whigs ultimately reduced the power of the Crown by the Reform Bill, and by instilling their doctrines into the youthful Queen Victoria. But in 1792 they had no remedy. Those of them who would not follow Burke into the Tory camp found it impossible to dissociate themselves in the public mind from Tom Paine. For years he stuck to everything Liberal like a burr. Either you were for ' the good old King,' or else you were set down as a rebel and a Painite. The man in the street, as he gazed through the shop windows at Gillray's cartoons, began to think of the Foxite Whigs as people in red caps of liberty intent on beheading George III and setting up a ragged Republic.

---

[1] *State Trials,* xxiv. pp. 294–5.
[2] See *Creevey,* ed. 1903, i. 118–19.

At this stage in our affairs, in the early months of 1792, while the Second Part of the 'Rights of Man' was appearing, and men were choosing their sides at the dictation of the most extravagant hopes and fears about the new era, two societies sprang into being, the outcome of that year's turmoil of all England thinking. Thomas Hardy, the shoemaker, founded the Corresponding Society, while Grey and his young Parliamentary allies founded the Friends of the People. Both societies were short-lived, but one of them was the origin of the future Radical, and the other of the Whig-Liberal party. They stood for two principles of progress familiar in English history—the people helping themselves, and a minority of the governing class helping the people.

Thomas Hardy's Corresponding Society was the first political and educational club of working men. It supplied the natural leaders of that class with the opportunity to emerge and lead, with the means of study and debate, and with an embryo organisation. There was then little Trade Union life except of a purely economic character ; no Co-operative Society life, and no higher education for the working class ; and therefore the Corresponding Society was as important in its moral and intellectual as in its political aspects. If it had not been crushed by the authorities, it would have done a still greater work and would early have stimulated other movements in working-class life, that began many years too late. Its political programme was Universal Suffrage and Annual Parliaments—that, and nothing more.[1] Its members did, in fact, circulate Paine's works, and most of them were theoretically Republicans ; but it was Parliamentary Reform that they worked for as the practical object.

Hardy and his friends were Londoners. London was then more Radical than the North, perhaps because

[1] *Place Papers*, Add. MSS., B.M., *passim*, e.g. 35142, ff. 236–7 ; 27814, ff. 31–2. Wallas' *Place*, Veitch's *Genesis of Parliamentary Reform*, and P. A. Brown's *French Revolution in English History*, 1918.

the Westminster and Middlesex elections, held on a
democratic franchise and enlivened by Wilkes and by
Fox, had accustomed the inhabitants of the capital to
watch real political contests, unknown in most towns
before the Reform Bill. At this time the working
men in Lancashire were still for ' Church and State ' ;
the year after the Birmingham riots the Manchester
mob imitatively wrecked houses of Dissenters and
bourgeois Reformers. But the Tom Paine movement,
working through the Corresponding Society and the
somewhat more middle-class Society for Constitutional
Information, acted from London, Sheffield, and Norwich
on the rest of England, and sowed broadcast the ideas
that re-emerged in the days of Peterloo as the Radical
creed of the working men in Lancashire and the industrial north.

Such were the origins of the new Tory and of
the Radical parties, between which Grey spent the
rest of his life in steering a middle course. Under the
impulse of the French Revolution, Burke had been able
to indoctrinate the governing classes with the theory
on which they acted for the next generation, namely,
that the British Constitution was not only perfect, but
unalterable ; and that everyone who advised his countrymen to alter it was a proper subject for ' criminal
justice.' Meanwhile Paine and Hardy had roused a
portion of the working classes to demand Universal
Suffrage, with the avowed purpose of improving the
lot of the poor, and a more vague intention of some
day establishing a Republic. In the long middle years
of his life, Grey with his Whig party was stranded so
precisely midway between this new Toryism and this
new Radicalism, that he had small influence on the
course of affairs. But in 1792-7, and again in 1830-2,
he was more nearly allied to the Radicals than to
the Tories, and it was on those two occasions that he
made history.

The action from which the rest of Grey's life flows, and from which the Whig-Liberal party takes its origin, was the founding of the Friends of the People in April 1792. It was this that broke up the old Whig party on domestic issues, a year before the war with France. There had been no split in 1791, when Burke renounced his friendship with Fox on the floor of the House, in a heated controversy on the merits of the French Revolution. At that time the majority of the Whig Members, preferring Fox to Burke personally, regarded the views of both on the French question as extravagant, and refused to quarrel among themselves about the internal affairs of a foreign country. The incident had left Burke more angry and more isolated than before.[1] That year he left Brooks's Club, to which all sections of the party belonged. The split in the party itself did not come till twelve months later, when Grey founded the Friends of the People. It was that act of Grey's which drove the anti-Reform section under the Duke of Portland to concert measures with Pitt against their fellow Whigs. Fox was thereby compelled to choose whether in the future he would work only with the Reformers or only with the anti-Reformers of his party. He had hoped against hope to avoid making the choice, but he had no doubt how to choose, if choose he must.

In this matter of the Friends of the People Grey did not follow Fox, but Fox followed Grey, to protect him from the consequences of an action of which Fox approved the purpose but disallowed the wisdom. This is the meaning of the passage in Lord Holland's 'Memoirs,' where 'the nephew of Fox and friend of Grey' tells us that :

Mr. Grey felt additional attachment to Mr. Fox and zeal for his party, from an apprehension, suggested by his warm, susceptible, and generous temper, that much of the obloquy cast

[1] *Sir G. Elliot's Letters*, ii. pp. 7–9, 102–3.

on the party was founded on measures of which he had been the author, and from gratitude for the noble and unaffected disinterestedness and spirit with which Mr. Fox had vindicated his conduct and supported him against the aspersions even of some of his oldest adherents.

If Fox had declined to throw his shield over the Friends of the People, they and not the Portland Whigs would have had to go.   For Fox was the Whig party, with whomsoever he chose to abide.   In siding with Reform he destroyed his own career and his good name in the world, but he prevented the Whigs from becoming bottle-holders to the Tories, and so enabled England, many years after his own death, to obtain Reform without Revolution.

These transactions require to be followed in some detail.   Considering the importance in our political history of the founding of the Friends of the People, which broke up the Old and originated the New Whigs, it is curious how little record we have of the first conception of the plan.   Lord Lauderdale and Philip Francis were, with Grey, the moving spirits ; Grey put his name first on the list of the Associators [1] and acted as their Parliamentary spokesman.   But Grey himself has told us little about it.   In the very last years of his long life he repented of the action, on the ground that it had linked him with extremists, although he never repented of the principles of Parliamentary Reform, which alone the Society was founded to promote.   In his last illness (1845) he told his son that ' one word from Mr. Fox would have kept me out of all the mess of the Friends

---

[1] The ' Association ' and ' Associators ' are the words used for the Society of Friends of the People and its members in the correspondence and speeches of the year 1792.   It will be seen that the list of their names, about 150 in all, contains no one but ' gentlemen,' and that there were originally twenty-eight Members of Parliament, five of whom resigned in June.   Their full proceedings can be read in the *Wyvill Papers*, iii. Appendix, pp. 128–292 ;   pp. 128–31 give the list, and pp. 169–71 the five who were expunged from the list on resignation.

of the People, but he never spoke it.'[1]   But when, still in the fulness of his powers, he was introducing the Reform Bill into the House of Lords as Prime Minister, in 1831, he had spoken to their lordships with pride of his connection with the Friends of the People as ' not at all inconsistent ' with the great measure he was then proposing.[2]

We have two accounts of the inception of the Friends of the People prior to the official meeting at which it was constituted, on April 11.   There is on the one hand the hostile tradition of Holland House that represents it as an after-dinner freak of irresponsible young aristocrats.[3]   On the other hand there is the friendly narrative of Thomas Hardy the shoemaker, who had founded the Corresponding Society a few months before ; to him the foundation of the Friends of the People seemed the generous act of young men of rank, ready to lend a hand to the democratic movement beginning in the lower classes of society.   The view of Lord and Lady Holland, and the view of Thomas Hardy, may both have some element of truth, but, as is often the case, the more sympathetic account has the most real insight.   The list of some hundred and fifty original Associators contains many honoured names of men who were much more than boon companions engaged in a foolish freak.

The London Corresponding Society [wrote its founder, Hardy] were encouraged by such men [as the *Friends of the People*]

---

[1] On the other hand, in June 1792, only three months after the foundation of the Society, Mr. Thomas Pelham wrote to Lady Webster : ' Fox told me that he had never been consulted about it, and that, on the contrary, the Associators seemed determined *not to have any advice*, and particularly not to *have his*.   This I know to be true, for Lauderdale told me that they were determined not to consult Fox until they saw the probability of success, in order that he might not be involved if they failed ' (*Lady Holland's Journal*, i. p. 15, note).

[2] *Hansard*, Oct. 7, 1831, p. 313.

[3] Holland, *Memoirs*, i. 13–14 ; and *Lady Holland's Journal*, i. 101.

stepping forward in the same cause, professing to have the same object in view, which caused the people to flock in astonishing numbers to the *Corresponding Society* ; they began to be very sanguine in their hope of success by such a respectable number of members of the House of Commons coming voluntarily forward in that cause which we were embarked in.   The society of *Friends of the People* were likewise encouraged to proceed by such large numbers of the industrious lower and middle classes of society which were associating in London and various parts of the country for a reform in Parliament.[1]

Thus for a short while shoemaker Hardy's club of working men, each paying a penny a week, and Grey's association of gentlemen, each paying two and a half guineas a year, grew and flourished by indirect mutual encouragement, though without any actual communication.   And later in the year there grew up, in various cities of Great Britain, other democratic societies, answering in social and political character to the Corresponding Society rather than to Grey's association, but calling themselves ' Friends of the People,' in embarrassing compliment to that highly respectable body. The furious outburst of rage, in Parliament and among the upper classes generally, against Grey's association, can only be accounted for by the example these much-abused gentlemen set to the lower orders.   For, apart from the moral support which their mere existence as a society lent to the more democratic clubs, there was nothing that differentiated the Friends of the People from the Reform associations to which Pitt and the Whig chiefs had belonged without censure a dozen years before.   Not only did the Friends of the People not circulate Paine's writings, but they expressly repudiated his views.[2]   Their two objects were :

First.—To restore the Freedom of Election, and a more equal Representation of the People in Parliament.

[1] *Place Papers*, Add. MSS., B.M., 27814, ff. 32–4.
[2] *Wyvill*, iii. Appendix, pp. 149–69.

Secondly.—To secure to the People a more frequent exercise of their Right of Electing their Representatives.

They never had, either officially or actually, any other object. The language of their Address to the People of Great Britain, adopted on April 26, was unexceptionable. After quoting as their predecessors in the movement ' Mr. Locke and Judge Blackstone, the late Earl of Chatham, the Duke of Richmond, Mr. Pitt, and Mr. Fox,' they proceed :

The example and situation of another Kingdom [France] are held out to deter us from innovations of any kind. We say that the Reforms we have in view are not innovations. Our intention is not to change, but to restore ; not to displace, but to reinstate the Constitution upon its true principles and original ground. We deny the existence of any resemblance whatever between the cases of the two Kingdoms ; and we utterly disclaim the necessity of resorting to similar remedies. Our general object is to recover and preserve the true balance of the Constitution. These are the Principles of our Association.

Resolved unanimously :

That a motion be made in the House of Commons, at an early period in the next Session of Parliament, for introducing a Parliamentary Reform.

Resolved unanimously :

That Charles Grey, Esq., be requested to make, and the Hon. Thomas Erskine to second, the above motion.[1]

Four days later (April 30, 1792) Grey rose in the House of Commons to give notice of the motion for a Reform of Parliament to be introduced for ' the next session.' Since a whole year was to elapse before he brought in his motion, he only said a few words in thus giving notice, and those words were certainly not provocative, except to persons who had come there to be provoked. He quoted Mr. Pitt as his predecessor in Parliamentary Reform. ' It is of the utmost importance,' he said, ' that the House should enjoy the good

---

[1] *Wyvill*, iii. Appendix, pp. 129, 139–44.

opinion of the public and possess their confidence as a true representation of the people.' ' The loss of that character might produce all the miseries of civil commotion.' If there were those who wished to excite such commotion, he disclaimed all connection with them, and believed that ' the evils threatening the constitution can only be removed by a timely and temperate Reform.'

It was then that Pitt first appeared in the full character of alarmist. As soon as Grey sat down, the Prime Minister was on his feet, talking of ' anarchy and confusion worse, if possible, than despotism itself.' Reform in Parliament might be well enough if everyone agreed to it, ' but I confess I am afraid, at this moment, that if agreed on by this House the security of all the blessings we enjoy will be shaken to the foundation.' Then he turned on the Friends of the People : ' I have seen with concern that the gentlemen of whom I speak who are Members of this House are connected with others who profess not Reform only but direct hostility to the very form of government. This affords suspicion that the motion for a Reform is nothing more than the preliminary to the overthrow of the whole system of government.'

There was yet no question of an approaching war with France ; it was not alluded to as a remote possibility, and Pitt had two months before declared his expectation of fifteen years' peace. In accusing Grey of the intention to ' overthrow the whole system of government,' because he made a proposal for Parliamentary Reform in the same spirit that he himself had made it seven years before, Pitt was acting as ' factiously ' in his own party interest as ever Fox had done, and with a want of generosity that Fox would never have displayed.

The moment that Pitt sat down Fox leapt up to defend Grey, and the split in the Whig party had begun. In the following month of May the divisions among the Whigs were further increased by a Royal Proclamation